SMALL GROUPS:
Getting Them Started, Keeping Them Going

Michael Wiebe

InterVarsity Press is the book-
publishing division of
Inter-Varsity Christian
Fellowship, a student movement
active on campus at hundreds
of universities, colleges and
schools of nursing. For
information about local and
regional activities, write
IVCF, 233 Langdon St.,
Madison, WI 53703.

Distributed in Canada through
InterVarsity Press,
1875 Leslie St., Unit 10,
Don Mills, Ontario M3B 2M5,
Canada

ISBN 0-87784-157-8

Printed in the United States
of America

The New Testament lays great stress on the importance of personal relationships among believers. We are told to bear each other's burdens (Gal. 6:2), to encourage each other (Heb. 10:24), to be concerned for each other's interests (Phil. 2:4) and even to admonish one another (1 Thess. 5:14). All this obviously means more than merely having superficial acquaintances.

Knowing other people on this level requires real work on our part. It also involves the risks of opening our lives to others and possibly being hurt. Yet, when believers gather together, they are instructed to make the effort and take the chances necessary to develop relationships of deep sharing and caring. What is it about personal relationships that makes them an important part of the New Testament lifestyle, a part worth the work and the risks?

4 The New Testament Pattern

The Apostle Paul summarizes the purpose of meeting together: "Let all things be done for edification" (1 Cor. 14:26). The context of this passage deals with the gifts possessed by every believer and the function of these gifts in relationships among believers. Paul is very emphatic that these personal relationships are indispensable. Every believer is vitally important to all the rest, and no individual can disregard the importance of any other member of the church (1 Cor. 12:14-21).

One of the best known chapters of the Bible (1 Cor. 13—the "love chapter") is set in this context to describe the quality of personal relationships to be sought among Christians. Their expression through the spiritual gifts of the individual is to be characterized by love. The ultimate goal of all this? The edification of those involved (1 Cor. 14:26).

Paul elaborates on edification in Ephesians 4, again in a context of relationships (vv. 2-3) and spiritual gifts (vv. 7, 11). Edification, or "building up" (v. 12), is spiritual growth. Its goal is a unity of faith and of knowledge, spiritual maturity and ultimate-

ly the full stature of Christ himself (v. 13). **5**
The result is spiritual stability, a lifestyle of
love, and growing to be like Christ (vv. 14-
15).

This growth is what Paul has in mind
when he writes to the Corinthians, "Let all
things be done for edification." This is the
aim of our personal relationships: both
growing to maturity ourselves and encouraging the growth of others. The bearing and
sharing and concern for each other are such
important parts of New Testament Christianity because they are powerful influences
shaping the development of our spiritual
lives into the image of Christ himself.

How then are we to spawn these relationships and, so, this growth? Many formats are
possible. Large groups alone usually cannot
produce this type of intimate interchange. A
large group will probably include some people we know better than others, but there
may also be some whom we have never met.
Sharing more than superficial information
about our lives is difficult in this situation.
The intimate burdens and joys of life are
things which most of us do not particularly
want to broadcast publicly.

6   To achieve the level of edifying relationships described in the New Testament, smaller groups are almost essential. Often the open and honest sharing and the growth process which begins in small groups can overflow into a larger body. Small groups offer an opportunity to know fewer people more deeply. This leads to the mutual trust that allows us to share our lives with one another. Then we can truly bear each other's burdens and encourage and even admonish each other when necessary. This is what small groups are for: knowing ourselves and each other better through Bible study, prayer and sharing so that we can grow to be like our Lord and to know him more fully.

Jesus made it clear that a large crowd is not a requirement when believers meet together (Mt. 18:20). His own earthly ministry involved a small group out of the multitudes that followed him. In this small group eleven men grew to a deep knowledge of Jesus that allowed them to spread his ministry to the world. Two of the eleven (Peter and John), who were in an even smaller, more intimate group with Jesus (Mt. 17:1; Mk. 5:37; 14:33), later became the leaders of the early church.

Others, even those who opposed them, rec- 7
ognized that their character was the result of
having been in the small group of men
around Jesus (Acts 4:13).

The pattern of the early church itself
followed this example. Because of its rapid
growth (three thousand people the first
day!), the believers met both in large corporate worship and in smaller groups in homes
(Acts 2:41-46). As the church continued to
grow, the believers continued in this pattern
(Acts 4:4; 5:42). As we follow this example
today, complementing corporate worship
with meeting in small groups, our lives will
reflect the resulting spiritual growth. Others
will "recognize us as having been with
Jesus" (Acts 4:13) because of his work in us
through our brothers and sisters.

Starting Out
If you're interested in growing spiritually
with others, but you can't seem to find a
small group, maybe God would lead you to
begin one. Here are a few suggestions.

To begin with, successful groups are not
started by a committee but by people like
you and me who are interested in their own

8 spiritual growth and that of others. Don't be afraid to start a group. Pray about it, seek God's will about it, but don't be afraid. Trust the Holy Spirit to work to bring the people to the group that he wants.

A good size for a small group is two to eight people. Although as many as twelve is possible, with more than about eight people, some of the advantages (such as everyone participating fully) begin to disappear. Don't worry about starting small. If you can find just one other person who is interested, the two of you can begin meeting and ministering to one another, trusting God to increase the size of your group when he is ready.

Try to meet regularly but be flexible. Once a week or once every two weeks is good. Meeting less often makes communication difficult. Knowing someone's day-to-day burdens requires seeing him more than once a month.

When you first start a group and are inviting a few people, specify a trial period. For instance, agree to meet for four weeks in a row. After the first weeks evaluate the group to see if needs are being met. Then decide if you want to continue.

Like anything new a small group can be a
little frightening because we don't know exactly what to do or what will interest and help others. While there aren't any magic formulas for success, there are some concrete steps you might try.

At the first group meeting spend some time discussing the goals of the group, why each person came and what each wants to get out of the group. But don't do this every week. Start into something right away that will edify and encourage.

Looking in the Word

Studying Scripture together is an exciting way to let God speak to each person in the group and to the group as a whole. Choose a book or a topic in the Bible and see what you can learn together. A large number of Bible study discussion guides are available. If schedules permit, the entire group could visit a Christian bookstore together to choose a guide. (*Basic Christianity* by Margaret Erb [IVP] is a series of eight Bible studies which includes many helpful suggestions for leading each study.)

If for some reason a guide is not available

10 for the particular passage you want, don't be afraid (with prayer) to study the Scriptures on your own. Ask three basic questions as you look at a passage: "What does it say?" (find the facts—Who, what, where, when?); "What does it mean?" (interpret the facts— How do the facts fit together? Why is the author saying this?); and "What does it mean to me?" (apply the interpretation to our- selves— Is there a truth to believe, an ex- ample to follow, a sin to confess, a promise to claim?). Questions similar to these, adapted to fit the particular passage you are studying, can help reveal what God is saying in his Word.

After putting in a couple hours of prepara- tion, the discussion leader should be con- scious of a few basic guidelines which will improve the value of the discussion time itself:

1. Never answer your own question. If no one gives a response, rephrase the question or ask, "Is the question clear?"

2. But don't be afraid of silence. Give time for the group to dig for the answers. Remember it took a little time for you to find the answers.

3. Don't be content with just one answer. **11**
Always try to get more people to contribute
to the discussion. Ask, "What do the rest of
you think?"

4. Acknowledge all contributions. Never
refuse any answer. If a questionable answer
comes up, you may ask, "Which verse led
you to that conclusion?" or "That's an inter-
esting point. What do the rest of you think?"

5. Stick to the point and avoid cross-
referencing. If people try to go outside the
passage you've agreed to study, ask "Which
verse led you to that conclusion?" If someone
wants to discuss tangents or related pass-
ages, suggest you do that after the study itself.

6. Don't be afraid of controversy. It can
stimulate interest. Try to guide thought
rather than stifle it. You may not be able to
resolve questions, but don't let that bother
you. Not all Scripture is crystal clear.

7. Encourage the shy member by asking
direct simple questions involving his opin-
ion or choice.

(For a more detailed discussion of Bible
study methods, see *Leading Bible Discussions*
by James Nyquist from IVP.)

12 Looking to God

Praying aloud together is a very specific way of bearing one another's burdens as well as seeking God's guidance and blessings for your group. Sentence prayers, in which each person prays as often as he wants but each time only a sentence or two on a single topic, are one way of sharing together in a time of prayer. This gives others in the group an opportunity to add their prayers about that particular subject either silently or aloud. It doesn't allow one person to "exhaust" all of the requests in one long prayer paragraph. As several pray together about one particular request, our faith and assurance of God's concern is strengthened through each other.

This also has the advantage of putting little pressure on those who do not feel ready to pray aloud in the group. They are not pushed to come up with an eloquent, long-winded, "spiritual sounding" prayer to match everyone else's. People can just pray what is on their hearts. Times of silence between verbalized prayers provide an opportunity both for silent prayer and for appreciating the presence of the Lord of Glory in the stillness of your group.

Like everything else about small groups, **13**
the format of praying together should be flexible, depending on the needs of the group. Some meetings might include a brief prayer time near the beginning and another at the end to pray about what was learned during the meeting. Another week the same group might spend an entire hour or more praying together, either for a variety of topics or for one or two especially significant needs.

Bearing, Sharing and Encouraging

Bible study and prayer should be the basic foundation for any Christian group. They provide the direct communication between us and God, and will keep the group focused on him. ("Where two or three are gathered *in my name,...*" Mt. 18:20.) But there are other ways to promote communication between each other to help develop the edifying relationships which are important to our spiritual growth.

The most obvious way is simply sharing—not just talking—real sharing. It's all too easy to spend the whole time talking about the football game or politics and never truly share ourselves. The time is gone and

14 you don't know each other any better. One way to begin sharing is to ask a question such as:

"How did you become a Christian?"

"What has been your most significant spiritual experience since your conversion?"

"What person has had the most influence on your spiritual life?"

"Name one thing you really like about yourself."

"Name one thing you would like God to change in yourself."

The group leader can suggest one of these topics and let people answer as they want to. Don't be afraid of a long silence—let people think about their answers. It is usually best not to go around the circle if the group is new since this can put pressure on a shy member before he or she is ready. As time goes on, these questions and others you think of can open the way for more spontaneous sharing about personal experiences, needs and joys.

Reading a chapter from significant Christian books on individual growth and small groups during the week and then discussing (and *applying!*) the contents as you meet together can provide numerous ideas about

growing to spiritual maturity together.
Books such as *Body Life* by Ray Stedman and *Prayer, Conversing with God* by Rosalind Rinker offer many practical suggestions which are especially applicable to small groups.

How about singing? Use a hymn or short chorus that everyone knows. Or even buy or borrow some hymnals. If there is a piano or guitar handy, fine. But if not, just make a joyful noise together. Singing is also another way to encourage sharing by discussing what a particular hymn means. Perhaps someone in the group could even write a song for the group to sing.

Encouraging each other in Scripture memory is another ministry the group can perform. You could start every meeting with each person sharing a verse he memorized during the week and why that verse is important enough for him to memorize. (Several suggestions for effective memorization appear in John Alexander's *Scripture Memory 101* from IVP.) Another possibility, which is more challenging and yet more valuable in the long run, is to memorize larger parts of Scripture together. It is often helpful if every-

16 one in the group memorizes the same passage with each member being accountable to the group. A brief time can be spent during the meeting dividing into pairs and reviewing from memory the passage for the week.

Sharing and praying for each other in the area of personal evangelism are as important to the group as to each individual. A group that is completely isolated and ingrown can quickly become dead and stagnant. Talking together about the joys and frustrations encountered while sharing Jesus with others will help the group see that it has a purpose outside of itself: to strengthen each other for carrying God's good news to a dying world. Role playing in pairs (with one member of the group playing the part of a non-Christian and the other of a Christian) can help in learning to present the gospel clearly and boldly. Often a written group prayer list can be kept and used during the week to support each other in prayer for non-Christian friends.

The Target
"If you aim at nothing, you'll be sure to hit it." If you are in a group, it's important to

know what you are aiming at and why you
are meeting. Making goals will help in knowing what to study, what to pray for and how to spend your time together. Understanding the group's goals will help in evaluating how the group is progressing: Are the goals being met or is the group wasting time? Do routine patterns need to be replaced by activities which are more in line with the goals? Is each person growing to be more like the Lord Jesus?

As you discuss what goals the group should have, don't be too vague. Mention not only "to grow as Christians" but also in what ways. Possibilities are to grow in patience, in prayer, in being a better roommate or husband or wife and so on.

Goals can be both short- and long-range. For example, in memorizing Scripture together long-range goals could include memorizing a chapter over a period of several weeks. You can break this down to a weekly short-range goal of each person coming to the next group meeting having memorized three verses of the passage.

Because each Christian has a specific spiritual gift empowered by God for the

18 good and the edification of others (1 Cor. 12-14; Rom. 12; Eph. 4), discovering and exercising these gifts might be a goal of the group. If the purpose of everything we do together is our spiritual growth (1 Cor. 14:26), discovering and using our gifts should be a high priority. *Body Life* and the Scripture it discusses are good places to begin.

Members may also set a goal of learning how to lead a group with the long-range goal of dividing to start several other groups. Some of these might be with Christians and others might be evangelistic Bible studies with one or two Christians leading a group of non-Christians in a study of the content of the gospel.

In establishing goals for the group try to make them not only specific but also measurable when possible. For example, setting a goal of "reading chapter two of *Body Life* for next Tuesday" is obviously much more measurable than the vague goal of "keep reading in Stedman's book." The more measurable goals are, the more useful they are in determining the progress and serving as an encouragement to the people in the group when the goals are met.

There must also be a balance in the goals 19
that are established. They must be both realistic and challenging. Goals which are completely beyond the capabilities of some or all
of those in the group will only lead to frustra-
tion and loss of motivation when they con-
sistently fail to meet the goals. On the other
hand, goals that are so limited as to present
no challenge do little for spiritual growth.
People complacently remain at their own
comfortable level, never moving beyond
their well-established plateau. But a bal-
anced goal is both realistic enough to attempt
and yet challenging enough to stretch (and
grow) our faith in God's power working in
our abilities.

Most important, goals should be seen as
the link between the needs in the group and
the activities of the group. Meaningful goals
cannot be established in a vacuum but must
be based on the needs of people. For example, the goal of learning what Scripture
says about raising children is fine when it is
based upon a particular need. But it will not
make much sense in a group of singles.
Think and talk about the immediate needs of
the specific people in your group and set

 goals accordingly. There will probably be many more needs than can be handled at one time. Concentrate on a few which seem the most pressing and set goals based on these. Then build the activities of the group around those goals. A group focusing on the goal of each member learning to lead a Bible study might have a different member lead each week. A group whose needs (and, therefore, whose goals) center on prayer might decide to have the one member who is the most gifted in this area do teaching on this subject for a set period of time. Clearly defined goals can help the group's activities be flexible enough to meet the needs of the group and to help each person grow.

A small group should also keep in mind its relationship to the larger group, the campus fellowship or the local church. Goals can be established to help the small group members be better ministers to others in the larger group in teaching, in exhortation or in other areas.

Finally, as members determine goals, prayer, as always, is vital. We must be sure that the goals are being established by God. It is his group. Let the goals be his goals and

expect him to meet them by his power
through us.

The Cost

Besides establishing goals for the group, each member should have a clear idea of what is expected of him or her as a member of the group (Lk. 14:28-30). Much friction from misunderstandings can be generated, as well as disappointments from vague ideas and differing opinions of exactly what is supposed to be done. The expression of commitment to the group might be verbal or it might be a written covenant signed by all the members. The degree of commitment can range from mere attendance to a covenant which has considerable effect on each member's life outside of the meeting itself.

Here are a few ideas you may want to include in or add to your group covenant:

1. *A daily quiet time*. Small groups are not magic; a person who neglects to spend time daily with his Lord cannot expect any weekly meeting to keep him spiritually refreshed and growing. Neither can he expect to encourage and edify the others in the group. Individual quiet times are a necessity to the

 spiritual health of both the individual and the group as a whole.

2. *Regular and prompt attendance.* Members who come only occasionally not only minimize their own spiritual growth, but also hamper that of others. A member who casually misses several weeks and then returns expecting the rest of the group to go back to where he left off is showing great insensitivity. Habitually delaying the group meeting because of latecomers wastes the time of those who arrive promptly and shortens the actual meeting time.

3. *Prayer for each other.* Bearing burdens does not stop when the meeting does. Regular prayer for each other not only brings the burden constantly before our loving Father, but it also develops our awareness of and concern for each other's welfare.

4. *Meeting outside the group.* Getting together outside the actual group meeting is essential to knowing each other. We all look different in different settings. Sharing a meal together occasionally, enjoying a hobby together, conducting an evangelistic outreach (either with the whole group or just two or three at a time) or playing volleyball to-

gether can greatly enrich your relationships.

5. *Meeting in the group.* Commitment to the authority of Scripture and to the fact that we as members of Christ's body are important to each other are necessary starting points for Bible study and sharing within the group. An agreement to avoid gossip and friendly (?) put-downs is essential if the sharing is ever to progress beyond a superficial level (Eph. 4:29). To keep from wasting the time spent together, members must agree that the time is the Lord's time and the meeting is his. A short opening prayer immediately at the beginning of each meeting to specifically commit the time to him may be helpful.

Most people hesitate to make a commitment to anything which seems to extend for an indefinite length of time. The group might want to limit the covenant, say, for twelve weeks. This allows enough time for you to begin to function as a supportive fellowship. At the end of that time the covenant could be renewed by those who choose to or modified as needed. Reproducing several copies of a covenant and having each member sign one provides tangible evidence of

24   the group's desire to grow and support each other.

The guidelines outlined in a group covenant are not to be taken as a rigid, legalistic system imposed upon the members. Rather, they should be discussed, modified and finally agreed upon by all those involved. In this way the covenant becomes a liberating instrument, allowing each member to know exactly what is expected of him and how he can depend on the others in the group. The covenant can also be used when inviting a new person to join. It can give him a clear idea of what the group involves and help him decide if he wants to commit himself to it.

Guiding the Group

If you are thinking about starting a small group or if you are already leading one, it might be helpful to think about your own role. It is very important to remember that the leader's function is not to be "in control" but rather to help the group meet the goals which have been prayerfully agreed upon. The leader is to be a servant in helping others grow spiritually.

Flexibility is important here because it is **25** easy to get into a routine and stay there even when it does not meet people's needs. That is a sure way to dry up a group. If things seem to be going stale, pray about changing the format and trying something different. Look at the needs of the group and the individuals in it and plan accordingly.

Rather than having the same leader every week, some groups will find it better to rotate the leadership. Each week a different member could lead the group using his or her own ideas. Or possibly you might have two coleaders who share in leading each week, who alternate from week to week, or who take short two- to four-week turns leading. One advantage of having more than one leader in a group is the ability to divide if it gets too large (more than ten or twelve people).

If there are several small groups meeting in your larger context of church, campus or neighborhood, it is often helpful for all the leaders to meet together regularly to share and pray for each other as leaders. It also might be good for all the groups to meet occasionally to fellowship and share with each other as a larger body of Christ.

Whatever approach you take in leadership, remember: It is not your responsibility to control the group. That is the responsibility of the Holy Spirit. Your responsibility is to humbly and prayerfully be his instrument in serving the members by leading the group (1 Pet. 5:2-3).

Problems to Avoid

Small groups are often used mightily by God to glorify himself and to edify and mature his people. The small, informal group is an excellent setting to experience the powerful combination of intimate fellowship and Christian growth described in Ephesians 4:11-16. But there are dangers. Perhaps just because the small group can be such a powerful tool of God, Satan seems to actively interfere. If you are in a group or are thinking about starting or joining one, there are a few dangers prayerfully to avoid.

Even though sharing is an important part of these groups, we often hide behind superficial masks whenever we get together. This might be expected at first. But we must pray, both for ourselves and others, that the masks

will be taken away. Sometimes just one per-
son who is willing to be humble enough to
ask for help or to share a problem can open
up the group to an atmosphere of honest
sharing.

But don't expect others to be open and
honest with you if you are hiding your real
self from them. Make yourself vulnerable to
the group by sharing some part of your life
that is truly important to you but which is
not something you normally advertise publicly, such as a problem or failure. The idea is
not to share something merely for the shock
effect it might have on the group. The idea is
to honestly and sincerely communicate, "I'm
imperfect, I need your help, and I trust you
enough to share with you my real, imperfect
self." This attitude in only one person (*you*,
remember?) is highly contagious, enabling
the others to trust you. This vulnerability can
bring a small group to a whole new level of
mutual trust, sharing and growth.

The other side of the coin is the response
of the group when one member begins to
share the burdens he needs you to bear. Real
listening and a desire to understand and feel
his feelings with him will communicate love

28 and help develop openness. Making jokes about his need (to "cheer him up") or forgetting about his problem an hour after the meeting will kill any hope of honest, "unmasked" communication.

Another area of caution is, perhaps surprisingly, that small groups can develop very close friendships. We need to watch that the group doesn't become an exclusive little club. We need the diversity of the other members of the body. It's important to maintain and develop friendships with people outside the group. Without them even the best small fellowship becomes ingrown and self-centered and soon shrivels and dies.

Relationships outside the group can take at least two general directions: ministry to the larger group of Christians or outreach to non-Christians. Ministry to the larger group should include continuing commitments such as regular attendance at a local church. Special ministries might also be considered by the group such as planning and organizing a picnic or other social event for the campus fellowship. A small group could also minister together in outreach by conducting evangelistic discussions in homes or dorms.

A third potential problem lies in what might be called "the third meeting slump." The first meeting is usually marked by the enthusiasm of a new adventure, and this may continue for a while. But often by the third time the group meets, many members feel the fellowship is not everything they had expected, perhaps because it didn't burst forth full-grown overnight. This meeting may be marked by disappointment or even antagonism.

Just being able to identify this problem can be a help in itself. Pray together about it. Trust God to get you through. The group that survives this experience and is open enough to discuss the problem is always stronger as a result. When members see each other's true feelings, communication becomes easier and you can begin to work through solutions together.

Taking a Backward Glance

Because we are to be good stewards of our time, we should carefully evaluate how we spend that time. Any activity which is a poor use of the hours God has given us should be abandoned or changed for the better. This includes small groups. After an initial trial period of four or five meetings, and then at regular intervals every few months, a group should spend at least part of or maybe a whole meeting prayerfully evaluating its past experiences. The place to start is with the goals that were established at the beginning. Are they still based on the real needs of the people in the group? Have they been met? Has specific progress been made toward them? Have the activities of the group been directed toward these goals or does the group spend its time in other ways? Are the goals realistic? Do they need to be changed? What can be done differently in the future to better meet the goals of the group?

How healthy is the group itself? Are the members growing and reaching out to each other? Has the group become a special club, only interested in itself? Or is there concern and prayer for sharing Jesus with non-Christians? And how is the group helping each person to grow and better minister to others in the body as a whole?

What are the relationships like in the group? Is everyone still wearing a mask? Is honest sharing taking place? Is there a feeling of freedom to disagree and work out differences? Do the people know each other better than they did a month ago? Are burdens being borne by each other? Are the members supporting each other in keeping the group's covenant? Are people growing spiritually directly as a result of this group? Consider, talk and pray about these questions and others you might think of. Be sensitive to all those in the group and to what God might lead you to do to strengthen them.

Is it all worth the work? Is it worth the risk of being known? One might just as well ask, Is it worth it to become more like Christ and help others do the same? God desires his people to be built up. He has chosen small groups as one major way for us to be edified and to help others move closer to "the measure of the stature of the fulness of Christ" (Eph. 4:13).

For Further Reading about Small Groups
Deshler, G. Byron. *The Power of the Personal Group*. Nashville, Tennessee: Tidings Press, 1960. Helpful especially in the area of honesty and trust.

Hunt, Gladys. *It's Alive*. Wheaton, Illinois: Harold Shaw Publishers, 1971. Exciting and chal-

32 lenging overview of small group Bible study. Good motivation for people not convinced of the value and potential of small groups.

Lead-Out. Colorado Springs, Colorado: Navpress, 1974. Good handbook for leaders, including many specifics on formulating and using questions to guide discussion.

Nyquist, James. *Leading Bible Discussions.* Downers Grove, Illinois: InterVarsity Press, 1967. Very practical ideas on starting a group, studying Scripture and leading a Bible study.

Richards, Lawrence O. *69 Ways to Start a Study Group*. Grand Rapids, Michigan: Zondervan, 1973. Ideas on topics ranging from how to get a group started to suggestions for things to do on a weekend retreat together. Emphasis on creative sharing and encouraging each other.

Rinker, Rosalind. *Prayer, Conversing with God.* Grand Rapids, Michigan: Zondervan, 1959. Practical guide on conversational prayer, including specific obstacles and problems which might be encountered and how to overcome them.

Snyder, Howard. *The Problem of Wineskins.* Downers Grove, Illinois: InterVarsity Press, 1975. A book on local church structure which has several chapters with wider application on fellowship, spiritual gifts and small groups.

Stedman, Ray C. *Body Life*. Glendale, California: Regal Books, 1972. Detailed discussion on spiritual gifts and how to use them in the body. Includes practical suggestions on discovering your own gifts.